HOW Were dinosaurs different from other reptiles?

Om KIDZ
An imprint of Om Books International

Contents

How do we get to know about dinosaurs?

By studying fossils! We know all about dinosaurs from the fossils which survived over the millennium. Fossils are remains (bones) or impressions of prehistoric plants or animals embedded in rocks. Palaeontologists have found fossilized bones of dinosaurs and have reconstructed these bones to find out what dinosaurs looked like, how they moved and even, what they ate.

Pocket fact

The first dinosaur bone!
The first dinosaur bone was found in England, in 1676, by Robert Plot. At the time, he believed that the bone belonged to a "giant," but later on it was identified as a dinosaur bone. The first dinosaur bone to be found belonged to the Megalosaurus.

Find out

Who proposed the method to classify dinosaurs?

How many types of dinosaurs are known?

Hundreds of them! At present, over 700 different species of dinosaurs have been identified and named by palaeontologists. Also, these species have been divided into two groups named Saurischia (lizard-hipped) and Ornithischia (bird-hipped).

How are dinosaurs named?

Usually, dinosaurs are named after a characteristic body feature, after the place where they were found or after a person who discovered their fossils. A dinosaur's name consists of two Greek or Latin words (or combinations). The genus name is written first followed by the species name. For example, the name T. Rex is a combination of both Latin and Greek words, and means "King of the tyrant lizards".

Try this!

If you were to re-name the Tyrannosaurus Rex and Dilophosaurus, which names would you like to use?

Pocket fact

First found!
The first Dilophosaurus specimens were found by Sam Welles in 1942, in the Kayenta Formation in Arizona. The site was discovered by a Navajo, Jesse Williams, in 1940.

How did Dilophosaurus get its name?

From its skull! Dilophosaurus was a carnivore that lived in the early Jurassic period, around 190 million years ago. Dilophosaurus had an unusual feature—a pair of crests on its skull. It is from this feature that it gets its name, which means "two-crested lizard".

How long could a dinosaur live?

It varied from one dinosaur species to another! The lifespan of an animal relates in part to its body size and metabolism. Palaeontologists observed growth rings in the fossil bones of dinosaurs. Similar to tree rings, each ring in a dinosaur bone marks another year of growth. These rings show that the large herbivorous dinosaurs, such as the Brachiosaurs and Diplodocus, would have lived for 70–80 years whereas the smaller, meat-eating dinosaurs had a lifespan of 20–30 years.

Pocket fact

The largest-known dinosaur egg is smaller than the egg of the extinct Elephant bird of Madagascar.

Find out

How small was the smallest dinosaur egg ever found?

How were dinosaur babies born?

They hatched from eggs! Unlike mammals, dinosaurs did not give birth to their young ones; the female dinosaurs laid eggs, just like most reptiles and birds do. The study of fossils shows that some dinosaurs made nests using twigs and leaves, or dug holes in the soil or sand to place their eggs. A baby dinosaur may have pecked its way out of its protective shell with a specially designed egg tooth, just like baby birds do.

How did dinosaurs move about?

They walked and ran! Different dinosaurs moved around in different ways. Some walked on four legs (these are known as quadrupeds), and some on two legs (these are called bipeds). There were other dinosaurs that may have used two legs to run but they still walked and grazed on four legs. A few of the bird-like dinosaurs may have used their short, feathered arms to help speed up their running and perhaps to glide from trees to the ground. Dinosaurs probably used their tails for balance while moving and making quick turns.

Pocket fact

The fastest ones!

The fastest dinosaurs were the bird-like, bipedal carnivores (theropods) with long, slim hind-limbs and light bodies.

How fast could dinosaurs walk or run?

Dinosaurs lived several years before human beings came into existence, so it is difficult to estimate how fast they walked or ran. However, scientists have suggested a formula to measure fossil footprints and the size of the dinosaur's leg to estimate the speed of some dinosaurs. As per the calculations based on this formula, the fastest dinosaurs were the ornithomimids, which ran at a speed of 25 mph. The walking-speed of medium-sized, two-legged dinosaurs varied from 4 kph to 6 kph, and for fast running dinosaurs, speed estimates were 37 kph to 88 kph.

Find out

Were there any dinosaurs that could swim?

How did dinosaurs fly?

They couldn't fly! The legs of dinosaurs were positioned under their bodies rather than out of the sides of their bodies (like that of crocodiles). So, what you might have assumed were flying dinosaurs were actually flying reptiles, known as pterosaurs. Examples of pterosaurs are Pteranodon and Pterodactylus. Aside from prehistoric insects, pterosaurs were the first-known flying reptiles.

Pocket fact

I weigh 100 grams!
Not all flying reptiles were huge like the giant dinosaurs. A pterosaur named Peteinosaurus, had a wingspan of less than 1 metre and weighed just 100 grams.

Find out

Where do palaeontologists look for dinosaur fossils?

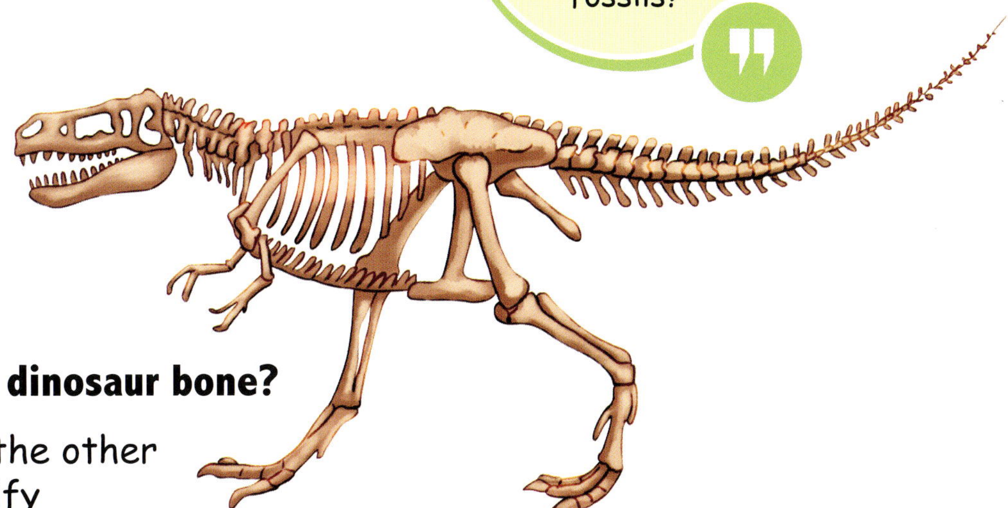

How do scientists know if they've found a dinosaur bone?

By comparing the shape of the bones with the other dinosaur fossils. Palaeontologists can identify the dinosaur bones on the basis of their size and characteristics. For example, dinosaur bones are usually larger than the bones of other animals belonging to the Jurassic age and they look different, particularly the skull and the pelvis. Also, meat-eating dinosaurs had hollow bones that were, usually, thicker than those of other birds or pterosaurs.

How many teeth did dinosaurs have?

The number varied from fifty to hundreds of them! The T. Rex had around 50–60 thick, conical, bone-crunching teeth. While the Hadrosaurus had the most number of teeth, up to 1000 cheek teeth that were like grinding machines. Unlike humans who only get two sets of teeth in their lifetime, a dinosaur's teeth would re-grow every time it lost them.

Pocket fact

I can't chew!

The dinosaur Apatosaurus had teeth but it couldn't chew. The American Museum of Natural History states that the Apatosaurus had "stripper teeth" that just removed leaves from branches. The dinosaur just swallowed plants whole without chewing.

Find out

When were the first dinosaur teeth fossils discovered?

How big was Tyrannosaurus Rex's longest tooth?

About 12 inches long! T. Rex had a mouth full of serrated teeth. But not all of the T. Rex's teeth were long and served the same function. The front teeth of a T. Rex gripped and pulled, its side teeth tore flesh and its back teeth diced chunks of meat and forced food into its throat. The T. Rex had wide and dull teeth, rather than flat and dagger-like, which allowed the teeth to withstand the forces exerted by the struggling prey. The longest T. Rex tooth ever found was about 12 inches (30 centimeters) long.

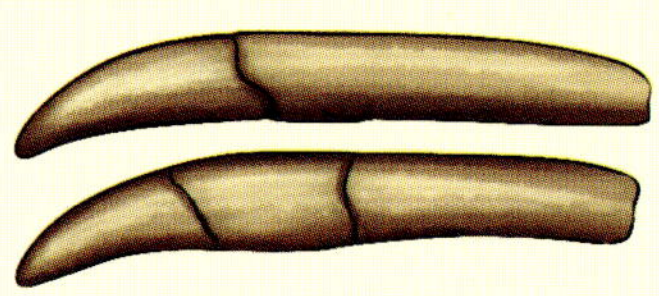

Find out

How did the Spinosaurus get its name?

How was the Spinosaurus different from the other dinosaurs?

Its size and some of its specific features made it different from the other dinosaurs! Spinosaurus was the biggest of all carnivorous dinosaurs and it mostly ate fish. Most meat-eating dinosaurs had curved teeth but the Spinosaurus had powerful jaws with straight teeth. It lived on both land and water and is said to be the only true aquatic swimming dinosaur. This dinosaur had an amazing sail made from spike-shaped bones, joined together by a layer of skin, on its back, hence the name Spinosaurus.

Pocket fact

Is there danger?
The Triceratops had a frill around its neck. It used this thin flap of skin to communicate with members of its herd. This frill also helped the dinosaur regulate its body temperature.

How many horns did Triceratops have?

Three! Triceratops was a huge plant-eating dinosaur from the late Cretaceous. Triceratops gets its name from the three horns present on its head. However, it actually had only two proper horns which could grow up to 3 feet long. The third horn was made out of soft proteins and wasn't a proper horn. It is said that the dinosaur used its horns to protect itself from danger.

How did dinosaurs turn into fossils?

When they died and got buried in mud and sand! Fossils are the remains or impressions of a prehistoric plant or animal embedded in rock. When dinosaurs died and got buried in mud or sand, the soft parts of their body were decomposed, leaving only the bones. Minerals from the mud soaked into the bones and gradually these minerals started replacing the bones. This turned the bones into fossils.

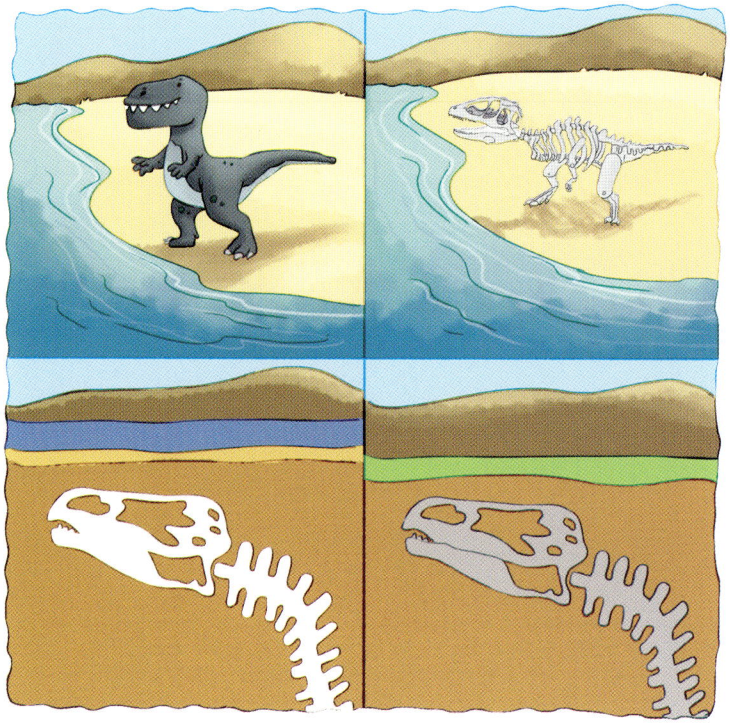

Find out

Which was the most ferocious dinosaur?

How did dinosaurs protect themselves from danger?

Different dinosaurs used different methods of defence! Some dinosaurs had sharp teeth, claws and whip-like tails that they used as weapons while other dinosaurs, like the Ceratosaurus, had horns for self defence. For speedy dinosaurs, being able to out-run a predator was their main means of protection. Large Sauropods used their size to frighten their enemies. On the other hand, the dinosaurs that did not have horns or spines may have relied on camouflage to protect themselves.

Pocket fact

Dug up!

The word fossil comes from the Latin word *fossilis*, which means, "dug up". Fossils are mostly excavated from sedimentary rock layers.

How are dinosaurs grouped?

On the basis of their bones! Scientists have classified dinosaurs into two groups on the basis of the structure of their bones. The most important difference between these two groups lies in the shape of their hip joints. Dinosaurs with pelvic hips, such as those of lizards, are called Saurischia. While, the second group called Ornithischia, comprises dinosaurs that have hip bones, similar to those of birds.

Pocket fact

Two names!

T. Rex was mistakenly named both "Tyrannosaurus Rex" and "Dynamosaurus imperiosus" by palaeontologist H.F. Osborn in his 1905 paper, after he found two fossils. He later realized that they were one and the same.

Find out

Which was the biggest plant-eating dinosaur?

How were plant-eating dinosaurs different from meat eaters?

There were many features that made them different! Plant-eating or herbivorous dinosaurs usually had long necks which helped them reach the tree tops and munch on the tree leaves. Most of them walked on four legs. They had horns, bony frills, plates, spikes, clubs and long tails. Their teeth were flat. On the other hand, meat-eating or carnivorous dinosaurs had sharp teeth and claws. Most carnivorous dinosaurs stood on two legs so that they could run fast to catch their prey.

How were dinosaurs different from other reptiles?

The difference lies mainly in the bones! Though dinosaurs were a part of a large group of reptiles, they were quite different from the present day reptiles. Reptiles have two vertebrae in their hips whereas dinosaurs had five. Reptiles, such as lizards and crocodiles, have their thigh bones almost parallel to the ground, with legs that sprawl out to the side, enabling a side-to-side motion. Dinosaurs, on the other hand, had a hole in their hip socket that helped them stand straight. This posture also allowed dinosaurs to run faster and with greater endurance than other reptiles of the same size.

Find out

How heavy was the heaviest dinosaur?

Pocket fact

We are a part of this group! The dinosaurs were a part of a large group of reptiles called the Archosaurs. The word Archosaurs means 'ruling lizard'.

How is the weight of dinosaurs measured?

It's not measured but estimated! The estimates are made by comparing the size of the dinosaurs with those of the similar present day animals. The estimates are made based on the width of the skeleton, the heaviness of the bones and the size of the dents in the bones where the muscles were joined to it. This also helps scientists to estimate the weight of a dinosaur's muscles.

Find out

Which was the most intelligent dinosaur?

How did dinosaurs communicate?

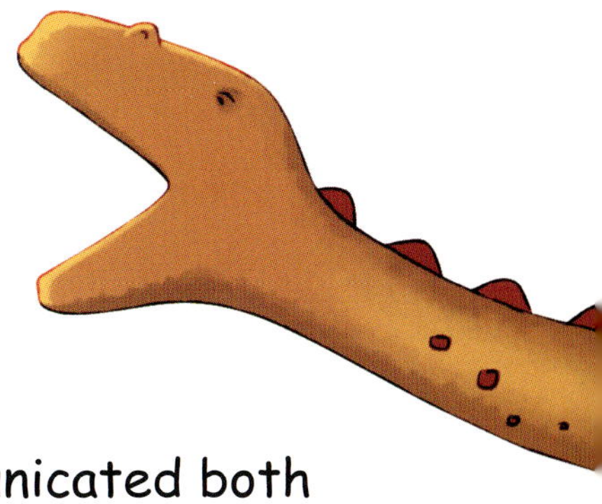

Dinosaurs probably communicated both vocally and visually. Dinosaurs such as Corythosaurus and Parasaurolophus had chambered head-crests which they might have used to grunt or bellow. Dinosaurs may have also used their horns, frills and crests for mating rituals or to intimidate rivals.

How big was a dinosaur's brain?

Some were walnut-sized and some the size of a tennis ball! Many of us are under the assumption that huge dinosaurs had large brains but this is not true! The size of the brain varied from one dinosaur to another. Troodon, a meat-eating dinosaur was the size of a 10 year old, with a brain the size of an avocado pit. Stegosaurus was a tiny-brained dinosaur, compared to its size. Its brain was the size of a walnut and its body was the size of a truck!

Pocket fact

It's the EQ!

Palaeontologists measure an animal's intelligence on the basis of EQ or Encephalization Quotient. EQ is the ratio of actual brain weight to the predicted brain mass for an animal of a given size.

How fast could dinosaurs grow?

They showed yearly periods of rapid and slow growth! Earlier palaeontologists generally assumed that dinosaurs grew slowly and required 50–100 years to attain their great size. But a recent study of growth lines in the fossil bones reveals that dinosaurs grew rapidly in their first years and then showed slow growth. Can you believe that the huge T. Rex grew to its full size, attaining a weight of 10,000 pounds, in 18 years? In order to obtain its immense size and weight, it could put on almost five pounds a day during its phase of maximum growth!

Pocket fact

From short to long!
Dinosaurs were found in different sizes—as tiny as rabbits to as massive as trucks lined together. The Micropachycephalosaurus had a long name but was just the size of a rabbit. On the other hand, the Antarctosaurus was about 59-feet long.

Find out

Which group of dinosaurs did the Baryonyx belong to?

How was Baryonyx a special dinosaur?

It shared many characteristics with crocodiles. Baryonyx is one of the strangest dinosaurs, yet discovered. It was a massive hunter that lived in or near water and hunted fish and other small animals. It had about 90 short teeth which lined its long mouth. Its most distinctive feature was a very large claw (about 12-inches long), which could be used both for protection against enemies as well as a useful tool for hunting.

How are birds and dinosaurs similar?

There were several similarities between birds and dinosaurs. Palaeontologists have found some dinosaur fossils that look almost exactly like birds. It seems these dinosaurs had hollow bones, similar hips, similar hands (modified as wings in birds, but same skeletal structure) and feet. Some other similar characteristics include their skull structure and the fact that they walk on two legs.

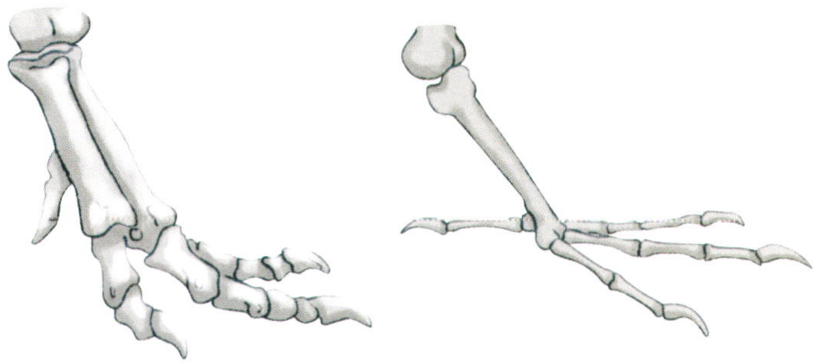

Find out

Were dinosaurs cold-blooded like reptiles or warm-blooded like mammals?

Pocket fact

The ancient wing!
Archaeopteryx which first appeared in the Jurassic period had the features of both birds and dinosaurs. It had a toothed jaw, clawed fingers, a long bony tail like a dinosaur but it also had a beak, wings and feathers like a bird.

How were pterosaurs and dinosaurs different?

Pterosaurs were flying reptiles that flourished during the time when dinosaurs lived. Pterosaurs were quite different from dinosaurs. Most pterosaurs had elongated jaws with needle-like teeth. Some of them also had a beak but lacked teeth. On the other hand, dinosaurs couldn't fly and each kind of dinosaur had different types of teeth. Plant-eating dinosaurs had flat teeth while meat-eating dinosaurs had sharp teeth. Also, pterosaurs are more closely related to birds than to reptiles.

Index